NATIONAL
GEOGRAPHIC

Chinese Immigration

IMMIGRATION TO THE UNITED STATES

Murray Pile

PICTURE CREDITS
Cover: a proud father, Chinatown, San Francisco © Picture History.

page 1 © Bettmann/Corbis/Tranz; page 4 (bottom left)
© Bettmann/Corbis/Tranz; page 4 (bottom right) © Corbis/Tranz;
page 5 (top) © The Granger Collection, New York; page 5 (bottom
left) © Ted Streshinsky/Getty Images; page 5 (bottom right)
© Bettmann/Corbis/Tranz; page 6 © Bettmann/Corbis/Tranz;
page 8 © Corbis/Tranz; page 9 © Underwood & Underwood/
Corbis/Tranz; page 10 © Hulton Archive/Getty Images; page 12
© Bettmann/Corbis/Tranz; page 13 © Picture History; page 14
© Bettmann/Corbis/Tranz; page 15 © Douglas Peebles/Corbis/
Tranz; page 16 (left) © Anthony P. Bolante/Reuters/Stock Image
Group; page 16 (right) © Mike King/Corbis/Tranz; pages 21,
23–25 © courtesy of Fiddletown Preservation Society, Inc.;
page 26 (left) © California Historical Society; page 26 (right), ©
courtesy of Dr. Herbert Yee; page 29 © Jose Luis Pelaez, Inc./
Corbis/Tranz.

Special thanks to Dr. Herbert Yee for his information on Yee
Fung Cheung.

Produced through the worldwide resources of the National
Geographic Society, John M. Fahey, Jr., President and Chief
Executive Officer; Gilbert M. Grosvenor, Chairman of the Board;
Nina D. Hoffman, Executive Vice President and President, Books
and Education Publishing Group.

PREPARED BY NATIONAL GEOGRAPHIC SCHOOL PUBLISHING
Ericka Markman, Senior Vice President and President, Children's
Books and Education Publishing Group; Steve Mico, Vice President
and Editorial Director; Marianne Hiland, Executive Editor; Richard
Easby, Editorial Manager; Jim Hiscott, Design Manager; Kristin
Hanneman, Illustrations Manager; Matt Wascavage, Manager of
Publishing Services; Sean Philpotts, Production Manager.

EDITORIAL MANAGEMENT
Morrison BookWorks, LLC

PROGRAM CONSULTANTS
Dr. Shirley V. Dickson, Program Director, Literacy, Education
Commission of the States; Margit E. McGuire, Ph.D., Professor of
Teacher Education and Social Studies, Seattle University.

National Geographic Theme Sets program developed by Macmillan
Education Australia, Pty Limited.

Published by the National Geographic Society
1145 17th Street, N.W.
Washington, D.C. 20036-4688

ISBN(Single): 0-7922-4751-5

ISBN(8-Pack): 978-14263-62194

Printed in Hong Kong.

2010 2009
5 6 7 8 9 10 11 12 13 14 15

Contents

Immigration to the United States

Do you know anyone who has come to live in the United States from a different country? People who immigrate to the United States do so for many different reasons. Some come for better work opportunities. Others want the right to have a say in their government or to live in peace. Still others want to practice their religion freely. Groups who have immigrated to the United States include Irish, Chinese, Mexican, and Jewish people.

 ## Key Concepts ....

1. People choose to immigrate for many different reasons.
2. People who immigrate face many challenges.
3. People who immigrate contribute to the life and culture of the society they join.

Four Groups of Immigrants

Irish

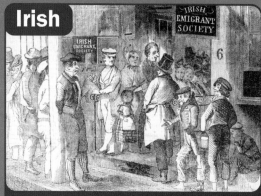

Many Irish people immigrated to the United States in the 1800s.

Chinese

Many Chinese people immigrated to the United States in the 1850s.

In this book you will learn about Chinese immigrants who came to the United States in the 1850s.

Mexican

Many Mexican people immigrated to the United States in the 1940s and 1950s.

German-Jewish

Many German-Jewish people immigrated to the United States in the 1930s.

Chinese Immigration
in the 1850s

What is it like to live through war in your own country? What is it like to always be hungry? Would you leave your country to look for work in a new land? This is what many young Chinese people did in the 1850s. They left China and traveled to America. They hoped to earn money to send to their families.

Background on China

China is a large country in East Asia. In the mid 1800s, China had terrible weather problems. People could not grow enough food to eat.

There were also many poor people living in China. They did not earn enough money to feed their families. The poor people did not like the way China's rulers were running the country.

Poor Chinese in the 1800s, plowing and sowing a field

In 1848 gold was found in California. Many Chinese, most of them young men, sailed across the Pacific Ocean to the United States. These young men wanted to make their fortunes. They wanted to find gold or a job in the United States.

Look at the map below. It shows the route the people had to travel from southeast China to California.

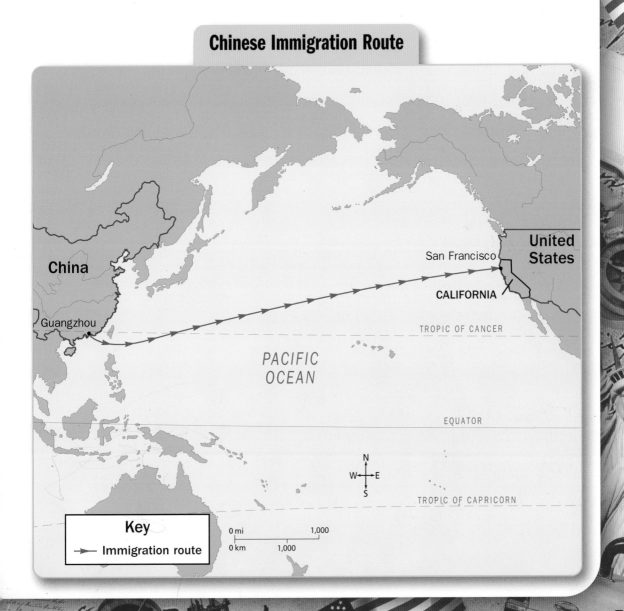

Chinese Immigration Route

China

Guangzhou

PACIFIC OCEAN

TROPIC OF CANCER

EQUATOR

TROPIC OF CAPRICORN

San Francisco

CALIFORNIA

United States

N
W E
S

Key

→ Immigration route

0 mi   1,000
0 km   1,000

Leaving China for Peace and a Better Life

Chinese people had many reasons to leave China and **immigrate** in the nineteenth century. The main reason was that life in China was so hard.

immigrate
to come to a new
country to live

In the mid 1800s, weather conditions made life very difficult. The Yellow River, a long river in north China, flooded farmland. In other parts of China, a **drought** dried out and killed food crops. The floods and drought led to **famine** in China. Many people were starving.

Around this time, there was also a civil war in China. A civil war is a war between groups of people in the same country. The war lasted 14 years and killed 20 million people.

Chinese chiefs and soldiers during the civil war

Flooding, drought, and war had badly damaged the countryside. There was a shortage of land for growing food. One area of southeast China, the Pearl River Delta area, still had good land for growing food. Many people went there. Soon the Pearl River Delta area became overcrowded. People then decided to leave China.

The stories about gold in California also made people want to leave China. Many **peasant** farmers from the Pearl River region decided to go to the United States. They saw the United States as a place of **prosperity.**

The Pearl River in China

The Challenge of Immigration

It is never easy to immigrate to a new land. The Chinese faced many **challenges** traveling to the United States. They faced more challenges when they arrived.

challenges
things that make life more difficult

The Journey from China

When gold was discovered in California, Chinese shipowners saw a chance to make money. The shipowners spread news about the gold in California. They offered tickets for the journey from China to the United States. Many Chinese wanting to go to California were poor. Most had to borrow money to pay for the trip. They planned to repay this money with money they earned in the United States.

Chinese immigrants arriving in San Francisco

Challenges in a New Land

The Chinese faced many challenges in the United States. They spoke a foreign language. They also looked different from many Americans. As a result, they were not always accepted by American people.

Many Chinese people went to work in the gold mines. They worked in mines that others had given up on. By working long hours, the Chinese miners often managed to find gold in these mines. American miners started to become jealous of the success of the Chinese miners. At several mines, they attacked Chinese miners and drove them away.

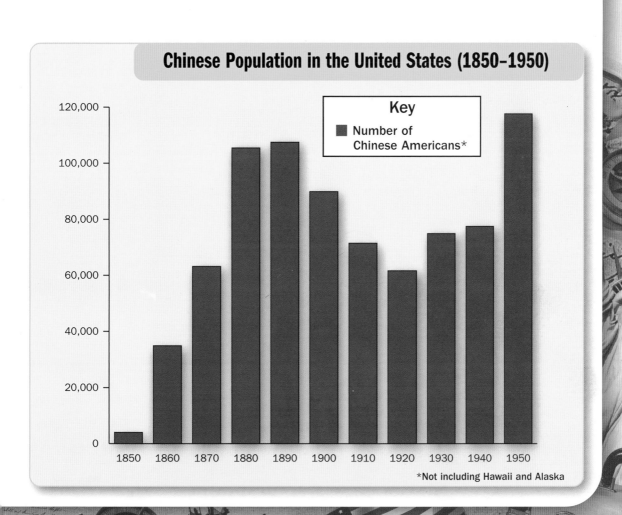

Chinese Population in the United States (1850–1950)

Key
■ Number of Chinese Americans*

*Not including Hawaii and Alaska

The Chinese also found other jobs in the United States. They worked as cooks, servants, carpenters, and laborers. By the mid-1850s, the gold had almost run out. Miners returned from the mines to go back to their old jobs. When they could not find work, they blamed the Chinese for taking the jobs. Soon, people began to blame the Chinese for anything that went wrong.

The Chinese were now met with strong dislike. At this time non-whites had no rights in a court of law. They could not give evidence against white people. Thousands of immigrants had no protection under the law. There were violent riots against the Chinese.

This illustration shows an anti-Chinese crowd attacking Chinese in 1880.

In the late 1800s the United States decided to stop Chinese people from coming to the United States. The Chinese Exclusion Act of 1882 **banned** new Chinese immigrant laborers from entering the country for ten years. Other laws continued this **discrimination** against the Chinese.

Few Chinese were allowed to enter the United States for the next 60 years. These laws were not changed until 1943. Then Chinese people living in the United States could become United States citizens.

A poster advertising an anti-Chinese meeting in 1885

Key Concept 3 People who immigrate contribute to the life and culture of the society they join.

Joining American Society

The United States is a country made up of immigrants. As with all immigrant groups, the Chinese have helped American **society**.

society
people living together in a group or nation

Chinese in the Workforce

One way the Chinese helped American society was through hard work. Chinese workers helped build the transcontinental railroad. This railroad linked the east and west coasts of the United States. The work was dangerous, and the pay was poor. Without the Chinese workers, the railroad would have taken years longer to complete.

Chinese laborers filling in land for the transcontinental railroad

Many Chinese farmers became farmers in the United States. They brought their knowledge of growing fruits and vegetables. Other Chinese had knowledge of fishing. They worked on fishing boats or in fish canning factories.

Chinese Culture in the United States

The Chinese also brought their **culture** to the United States. Chinese New Year is the most important time of the year for Chinese. Celebrations begin between January 21 and February 20. Many Chinese-American communities have festivals and fireworks at

culture
the traditions, language, dress, ceremonies, and other ways of life that a group of people share

Chinese New Year. The celebrations end with a parade. The festivals also include American-style marching bands and floats.

A Chinese dragon dance at Chinese New Year celebrations in Hawaii

The Chinese Contribution

Over the years, many Chinese-Americans have been very successful. Amy Chow competed in gymnastics for the United States. She helped her team win a gold medal at the 1996 Olympic Games. Her parents are Chinese immigrants, and she was born in California. Gary Locke, whose father came from China as a teenager, was first elected governor of Washington in 1996. He is the first Chinese-American governor in United States history.

Since 1940 many Chinese have come to the United States to live. Chinese-Americans are now one of the fastest growing ethnic groups in the United States. About 2.8 million Americans today claim **descent** from Chinese immigrants.

Governor Gary Locke of Washington State

Gymnast Amy Chow

Think About the Key Concepts

Think about what you read. Think about the pictures and the graph. Use these to answer the questions. Share what you think with others.

1. Why did the immigrants discussed in this book leave their country?

2. What were some challenges the immigrants faced when they arrived in the United States?

3. How did the immigrants overcome the challenges they faced?

4. How did the immigrants contribute to the culture of the United States?

Bar Graph

Bar graphs are used to compare different amounts.

A **bar graph** uses different bars to show amounts that are being compared. Look back at the bar graph on page 11. It compares the number of Chinese Americans in the population over many years. Each colored bar represents a different year.

The graph on page 19 is also a bar graph. It shows the population of different groups of people at the time of the 2000 Census. A census is when the government counts all the people living in a place.

How to Read a Bar Graph

1. Read the title.
   The title tells you what information the bar graph shows.

2. Read the key.
   The key tells you what subjects are being compared.

3. Get the general idea.
   On the bar graph, taller bars represent a greater quantity than shorter bars.

4. Get the details.
   Look at the numbers on the vertical line, or axis. These numbers help you figure out the exact quantity each bar represents.

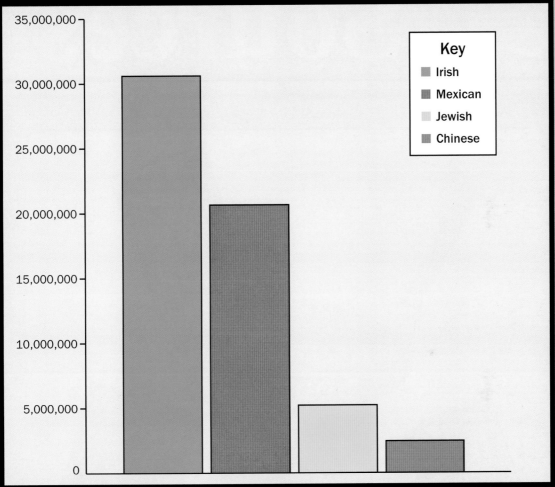

Key
- Irish
- Mexican
- Jewish
- Chinese

What Does the Graph Show?

Read the bar graph above. Then answer the following questions. How many Chinese people lived in the United States in the year 2000? What other cultural groups are shown on the graph? How many of each were in the United States population in the year 2000?

Biographical Sources

The purpose of **biographical sources** is to give information about people's lives.

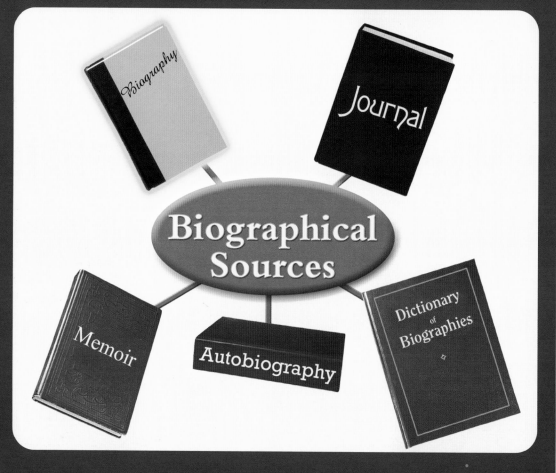

We read different biographical sources for different reasons. For example, if you want to read the story of someone's life, read a **biography.** If you want to read one person's account of his or her own life, read that person's **autobiography.** Journals and memoirs are forms of autobiographies.

A Biography of Yee Fung Cheung

1825–1907

The **title** identifies the person.

Dates tell when important events occurred, such as birth and death.

Photographs show the person, an event, or an important place in the person's life.

Yee Fung Cheung's restored herb store in Fiddletown, California.

Yee Fung Cheung was one of the thousands of Chinese immigrants who came to the United States in 1850. He practiced Chinese herbal medicine and became very well known in California. Yee treated many people, both Chinese and non-Chinese, for more than 50 years.

Text has details about the person's life.

Yee was born in Toisan, a city in China, in 1825. He followed in his father's footsteps by becoming a herbal doctor. Herbal doctors use tea made from parts of plants, such as leaves, flowers, bark, and roots, to treat their patients. They need a great amount of knowledge and skill to do their work. It is very important to get the balance of the mixture right to treat each illness.

During the hard times of poverty and war in China, Yee heard about the gold discovery in California. He decided to travel there in 1850. His wife, Chang Shee, and four children stayed behind in China. Yee arrived in San Francisco. He then traveled by steamboat to Sacramento. From there he made his way to a gold-mining camp near the town of Fiddletown, in Amador County.

Fiddletown was a trading center for mining camps in the area. There were many Chinese miners in these camps. Fiddletown grew into a large town. In 1860, 2,000 Chinese lived there. They worked in stores. They worked as carpenters and laundrymen. They had many other jobs, too.

A **timeline** shows key events in the person's life.

Timeline of Yee Fung Cheung's Life

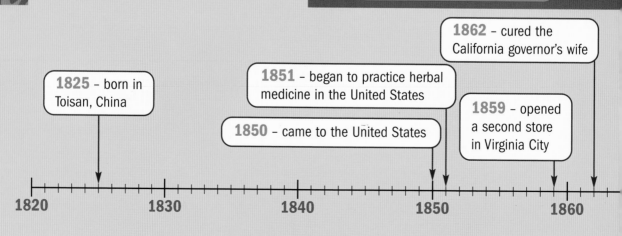

1862 – cured the California governor's wife

1825 – born in Toisan, China

1851 – began to practice herbal medicine in the United States

1850 – came to the United States

1859 – opened a second store in Virginia City

1820 1830 1840 1850 1860

Life in the gold-mining camps was very tough. Gold became harder to find. The people were unfriendly to the Chinese miners.

In 1851 Yee Fung Cheung gave up looking for gold. He decided to practice herbal medicine again. He imported medicines from China. They came by boat from Canton to Sacramento. Then they were carried by wagon to Fiddletown.

Yee's store, called the Chew Kee store, has been restored and is now a museum.

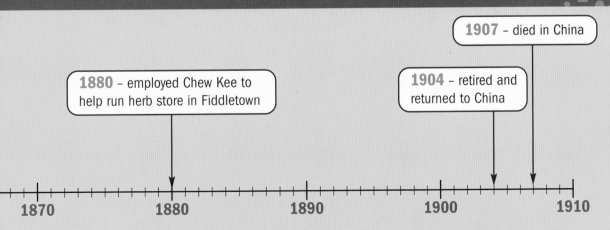

1907 – died in China

1880 – employed Chew Kee to help run herb store in Fiddletown

1904 – retired and returned to China

1870   1880   1890   1900   1910

The Chinese people of Fiddletown built a store for Yee. They used methods they had used in China. They made the walls by dumping moist soil between wooden forms, or molds. Then they rammed or hammered the soil until it became as hard as stone. The forms were raised and more soil added. Finally, the walls of rammed earth were the right height and about 3 feet (1 meter) thick. The front of the building was the grocery and herb store. Yee lived in rooms at the back of the building. There was also a little room for Yee to treat his patients.

Sickness was common in the gold towns, and Yee's practice was very successful. At first, he treated the Chinese from the local mines. His skill as an herbal doctor became widely known. He began to take care of sick people of all races and nationalities. Yee gained wide acceptance because of his skill.

A recent photograph of the inside of Yee's store

In 1859 silver was found in Virginia City, Nevada. Many gold miners went there. Yee could see that there would be people there who would need health care. He opened another herbal medicine store in Virginia City. A few years later, he opened a third store in Sacramento. There he treated workers on the transcontinental railroad.

Yee's consulting room in his restored store

One day in 1862, the state governor's Chinese cook came to ask Yee for help. Governor Leland Stanford's wife was very ill. Normal medical treatment had failed. Yee made up an herbal medicine that cured the governor's wife. The governor's staff did not know Yee's real name, so they called him Dr. Wah Hing after the store where they had found him. This was the name that non-Chinese called Yee Fung Cheung for the rest of his life.

In 1880 Yee employed a man called Chew Kee as a full-time assistant to help run the Fiddletown store.

In 1904 Yee Fung Cheung, the famous herbal doctor and California pioneer, retired. He returned to China, his country of birth, and died there three years later.

Yee's youngest son, Yee Lock Sam, had by then also come to the United States. He adopted the name Wah Hing and took over his father's business in California.

Mrs. Jane Stanford, the wife of Governor Stanford

Yee Lock Sam, who adopted the name Wah Hing

Apply the **Key Concepts**

Key Concept 1 People choose to immigrate for many different reasons.

Activity

Think about the reasons Chinese immigrants came to the United States. Create a two-column cause and effect chart. In the first column, list the causes of problems that led the Chinese to leave China. In the second column, list the effect of each problem.

Cause	Effect
shortage of good land	overcrowding

Key Concept 2 People who immigrate face many challenges.

Activity

Imagine you are a Chinese immigrant who arrived in the United States in the 1850s. Write a letter to a friend who is planning to immigrate to the United States from China. Explain the challenges you have faced since immigrating and offer advice to help the person know what to expect.

Dear Cheung,
I arrived in the United
States one month ago...

Key Concept 3 People who immigrate contribute to the life and culture of the society they join.

Activity

Think of some of the contributions made by Chinese immigrants. How did they help American society? Draw a word web and name the major contributions.

Farming skills

Chinese contribution

Write a Biography

Biographies are usually written about well-known people. They can also be about someone you know personally. Now you will write a biography. The biography will focus on important events and facts about a person's life.

1. Study the Model

Look back at pages 21–26. What are the things you need to think about when writing a biography? You will need to remember these as you write. Now, read the biography again. Look at the timeline. List the types of events that are mentioned.

Writing a Biography

◆ Choose a well-known person or someone you know personally.

◆ Write about events in the person's life in the order that they happened.

◆ Try to use photographs of the person at different times in his or her life.

2. Choose Your Person

Choose a person to be the subject of the biography. You may choose someone you admire. You may choose someone well-known whom you would like to find out more about. You might like to choose a musician, a sports figure, a famous scientist, or another outstanding person. You may choose someone in your family or community.

3. Research Your Person

Find out about the important events in your subject's life. For a famous person, find books in the library or articles on the Internet. For a person you know, conduct an interview. Plan and ask questions to help with your biography. Remember to bring a parent or other adult with you if you interview your subject in person. Make a list of the major events in the person's life. Copy photographs that you can use to illustrate the biography.

Richard Lopez (Grandpa)

- Born in 1925
- Graduated from college in 1948
- Married Maria Smith (Grandma) in 1950

4. Write a Draft

Look over all the information you have. Tell about the important events in order. At the end, tie the events together in a concluding paragraph. Then draw up a timeline. Write a few words about the important events along with the dates they occurred.

5. Revise and Edit

Read over your draft. Does it read like an interesting story? Check all the facts and the dates. Look for misspelled words or incorrect sentences. Be sure you have the information in the correct order.

Present Your Biography

Now that you have written a biography, you can share your work with the class. Get ready to present your biography.

How to Present Your Biography

1. **Prepare an introduction and a summary.**
   To begin your presentation, you will want to explain why you chose to write about your subject. For the next part of your presentation, prepare a brief summary of your subject's life. Include their birth date and major things they did.

2. **Decide on key life events.**
   Choose three events from the biography that you think are the most important events in the person's life. You will explain why you think these events were most important.

3. **Practice with a partner.**
   Once you've decided on the information you will present to the class, practice your presentation with a partner. Use note cards if they are helpful to you.

4. **Make your presentation.**
   Now you are ready to make your presentation to the class. Be sure to speak slowly and in a clear voice, and look up often from your notes to your audience. When others are making their presentations, make sure you are listening carefully.

5. **Answer any questions.**
   When you have finished your presentation, answer any questions your classmates may have about your subject.

Glossary

banned – forbidden

challenges – things that make life more difficult

culture – the traditions, language, dress, ceremonies, and other ways of life that a group of people share

descent – the origins of a person's family

discrimination – treating people differently or unfairly because of their race

drought – a long period of dry weather

famine – an extreme shortage of food

immigrate – to come to a new country to live

peasant – a person who lives in a farming community, especially in poor areas of the world

prosperity – good fortune and success

society – people living together in a group or nation

Index